THE

LITURGY

EXPLAINED

THE
LITURGY
EXPLAINED

James Farwell

Morehouse Publishing
NEW YORK · HARRISBURG · DENVER

Morehouse Publishing, 4775 Linglestown Road, Harrisburg, PA 17112

Morehouse Publishing, 445 Fifth Avenue, New York, NY 10016

Morehouse Publishing is an imprint of Church Publishing Incorporated.
www.churchpublishing.org

Cover design by Laurie Klein Westhafer
Typeset by Beth Oberholtzer

Library of Congress Cataloging-in-Publication Data

A catalog record of this book is available from the Library of Congress.

ISBN-13: 978-0-8192-2838-3 (pbk.)
ISBN-13: 978-0-8192-2839-0 (ebook)

Printed in the United States of America

CONTENTS

Introduction
1

CHAPTER 1
The Sacred Geography of the Liturgy
11

CHAPTER 2
The Structure of the Liturgy
15

CHAPTER 3
What We Do in the Liturgy
19

CHAPTER 4
Bodies in Motion:
Gesture, Movement, Ceremonial
49

Conclusion
55

Introduction

The Eucharist is the entrance of the Church
into the joy of its Lord.
And to enter into that joy, so as to be a witness
to it in the world, is
indeed the very calling of the Church,
its essential *leitourgia,*
the sacrament by which it "becomes what it is."

ALEXANDER SCHMEMANN[1]

A story is told of a young man, an unsavory type, who falls in love with a saintly young woman. Knowing that she will not so much as look in his direction, he slips into the vault of the town cathedral, dons one of the masks of the saints used in the annual town festival, takes on the demeanor and behavior of a saint, and begins to woo her. Surely enough, over time, she begins to fall in love with him. As the relationship flowers and deepens, the young man's scoundrel friends finally become envious of his success with the saintly young woman and, one day, out of sheer spite, challenge him in the center of the town square, in the presence of his beloved, to take off the mask and reveal his true identity. Dejected, knowing that all is lost, he slowly removes the mask . . . only to reveal that his face has become the face of the saint.

The origin of this story is uncertain, the present author no longer recalling where he first heard it. Its inspiration, however, is clearly medieval dramas, eighteenth-century stories of the *masque,* and even St. Augustine's theological account of desire in our search for God.

1

Whatever its source, it is an apt metaphor for the function of liturgy in the best possible case.

The Liturgy is the shorthand term we use for the service of worship called, by various families of Christian faith and practice, The Holy Eucharist, the Mass, the Divine Liturgy, Qurbana, Communion, or the Lord's Supper. In due course we will explore the meaning of the liturgy, consider the use of *liturgy* as a term for the Eucharist, and reflect on its structure and the practices. But first, our story.

In the liturgy, the people who call themselves followers of God don a mask, as it were. In the liturgy, they enact in ritualized ways the actions and attitudes befitting those who are followers of the God of Jesus of Nazareth. In the liturgy, they praise the source of beauty and truth, listen to the proclamation of love and the laws of human flourishing in the kingdom of God, lament that which is broken in the world, focus their energy on help for those broken, acknowledge their failings and commit to begin again to seek God and the good, make peace with one another, and welcome one another to a shared table. Like the young man in the story, they seek the one they love, or try to love, or want to love more deeply, and they do so by behaving—again, in "ritual shorthand"—in ways that are congruent with the nature of the One they love. They bring their desires for God and for Life—sometimes focused and afire, though often enough halting, partial, and unfocused—and they direct their actions of worship, praise, lament, and prayer toward the object of their desire, the One from whom all good, mercy, and truth flow out into a broken but glorious creation of which they are a part. Ideally, over time, as they wear that mask of desire for God, ritually enacting peacemaking, welcome, intercession, and sociality, they become like that for which they long. They become more like the persons they aspire to be for the sake of the One they love.

There is deep wisdom to this story. As old as Aristotle's ethics and as new as modern moral and psychological theories is the understanding that we become the persons we want to be by first *acting* like the persons we want to be, even before we fully feel ourselves to be such persons. Too, the wisdom is there in the mask story that we become like what we desire, and so we do well to take care with our desire and place it, above all, in that which is most deeply worthy of being desired. Being clear about our highest, ultimate desire brings clarity and order to the many other desires we have.

Of course, like all stories and metaphors, the mask story has its limits. Liturgical action, at its best, is indeed like the actions of the young man who seeks to be in a loving relationship with the one he desires and who becomes more like her over time, winning her over in the end. But unlike the young man in the story, in the case of the liturgy, Christians are always already taking the *second* step in an unfolding narrative of love's emergence: it is, as St. Paul and St. John wrote, God who first loves, who IS love, and we whose love is first awakened and focused by the love we have received. Like Michelangelo's painting, God's hand reaches for Adam—for humanity, both women and men—and Adam reaches back, even if haltingly, responding to the divine initiative. Liturgy, as Robert Taft puts it, happens in the gap between the two hands reaching for one another: one in action, one in response.[2]

If the ultimate purpose of liturgy is an action in which human beings "practice" who they are, or desire to be, in response to the One who loves them first, then perhaps we can understand who Christians are meant to be by exploring the meaning of the term *liturgy*, looking at the structure of the liturgy, and reflecting on the practices that make up the structure. That is the purpose of this book: to explain the liturgy and, in the course of doing so, to linger over Christian identity itself.

What we will discover in our study is that being Christian—contrary to an unfortunate, and widespread, misunderstanding—is not really about *holding certain beliefs about God and the world*, but about *becoming a certain kind of person before God and in the world*. Being Christian turns out to have a great deal to do with being a person who is fundamentally grateful to God for life, committed to living in communion with others, and acting compassionately toward other beings, just as Jesus Christ has done. And liturgy has a great deal to do with becoming Christian.

To understand this, and before explaining the liturgy of the Eucharist, we might best begin by reflecting on the term *liturgy* in relation to several other terms to which it is related. After all, if the service of Holy Eucharist is called *the liturgy,* where does this term come from and what does it mean?

Ritual

Let us begin by considering a generic term to which our question is related: that term is *ritual.* All religious traditions involve rituals. Indeed, ritualizing is something all human beings do, whether they consider themselves "religious" in the narrow sense or not. We relate to the world, convey what we think is most important, and make our way through the passages of life through various rituals. Some rituals are religious (depending on how one defines "religious"); many are civic, or social, or communal. Rituals are seen as a dimension of activities as diverse as American Thanksgiving meals, football games, weddings both within and beyond faith communities, New Year's celebrations, and family gatherings of various kinds. Some rituals are loosely organized, like a Thanksgiving meal in which many of the same people will be involved from year to year; traditional foods are often (though not always) served; some (though not all) of the same family jokes and stories will be told; and the sequence of the day will be fairly predictable, though not rigid, involving, perhaps, elements of gathering and greeting; watching or playing of games; eating the foods associated with the ritual; and so on. Some rituals are more tightly organized and scripted, with specific words and actions, organized in a sequence that is invested with importance so that it does not change. Religious rituals are often of this more highly organized kind.

Our tendency to ritualize may at first be puzzling, or we may be tempted to dismiss the importance of rituals. In part this is because we have been taught since the sixteenth century or so to think of our identities as being centered in the thinking and willing part of ourselves—our souls or our minds. But we have bodies; in fact, we don't just *have* bodies, we *are* bodies. We are embodied beings, whether one understands that to mean that we are *souls in bodies* as some of our Greek intellectual ancestors tended to do, or *ensouled bodies*, as religious traditions like Judaism tend to do, or *bodies with consciousness*, as contemporary neurobiology and neuropsychology do. However we understand ourselves as embodied, our embodiment means that we signal our important values and beliefs, and navigate our most significant life passages, by the whole-body activity of ritual. Thus, rituals involve not simply words and intellectual reflection but ceremony and gesture, movement and song, sound and smell.

Sometimes we use the term "ritual" to mean anything we do on a regular basis, like brushing our teeth in the morning. But rituals are not merely things we do repetitively. We may brush our teeth in roughly the same way every morning, but we could do so differently, so long as our teeth get clean. Brushing our teeth has a utilitarian purpose. Rituals in the full sense of the term are done with a certain amount of repetition because they are scripted, figuratively or literally. They have a normative structure that is considered significant to the values or realities that they are aimed toward, and those values or realities are themselves considered significant in an *ultimate* way. Rituals are not simply utilitarian; they don't simply get something accomplished but situate the practitioners within a higher value or set of values that give life meaning. Ritualizing is centered on the beliefs or values that a particular person, group, or culture considers in some way central to their identity and flourishing. It is centered on them in the mode of practice, not simply by way of ideas.

Furthermore, rituals are not simply dramatic expressions of those central things we believe anyway or that happen to us elsewhere. While there are some exceptions, often enough rituals actually *enact* what we believe, bring to pass certain states of being. Everyone is familiar with a wedding or blessing of a lifelong relationship, and this is a good example of the way in which rituals enact reality. When a couple participates in a marriage or blessing ritual, they are not simply dramatizing a covenantal relationship that has already occurred, though certainly it has begun to take shape in the life of the couple. They are not just announcing something to the public in a particularly festive way. The couple cannot "believe themselves" into being married. Rather, in the course of the ceremony, the marriage itself is actually brought to pass. When the ritual begins, the couple has a relationship and an intention to make it covenantal and faithful and compassionate, but they are not married, no matter how much they wish or intend to be. Through the marriage rite, *they become* married; the ritual points to their relationship and their intentions for lifelong commitment, but it also brings to pass that to which it points.

Really, most rituals work in this way, and not just in Christianity, but there is a special term Christians use for rituals that bring to pass what they point to: *sacraments*. The line between rituals in general and sacraments in particular is not really absolute, but a sacrament is a core ritual and is used to refer to the materiality, the physical objects or signs through which ritualizing enacts identity. Sacramental materials are usually of an elemental nature: food, water, oil, for example. In some religious traditions, such as Hinduism, fire or other natural elements could be said to function sacramentally. In Christianity, in the ritual of Eucharist that concerns us in this book, the sacramental material is bread and wine. These are foods that, when used in the ritual of the Eucharist—handled, prayed over, and eaten in highly scripted ways—are taken not simply to remind people of Jesus, or even point to the risen Christ who gave his life as divine love for the world, but to make the risen Christ truly present in the lives of those who worship. The bread and wine are not divine; they are not Christ in a literal way; yet they are called the Body and Blood of Christ because in eating bread and drinking wine in this way, the Christ to whom the sacramental foods point is also made really present to the members of the Eucharistic community through the eating of those foods. Christians have had many ways over the years of explaining how the bread and wine convey the real presence of Christ. Here we will content ourselves with the observation that, ritually consumed, they bring to pass that to which they point: the continuing presence of the divine among the human community that desires God and seeks to live, like the young man in our story, in a way befitting the One we love—the One who first loved us.

Christians believe the sacrament of the Eucharist makes God present through Christ in this way we have described, not because the ritual itself contains some special power to do so, but because Jesus told his disciples, at the last meal eaten with them before his death, to eat bread and wine in this way in memory of him. The Jewish form of memory from which Jesus worked is one in which the past is not simply recalled but made present. So in the Eucharist, a ritual of thanksgiving to God ("thanksgiving" is roughly what the term *Eucharist* means), Christians offer praise to God, hear their sacred Scriptures read, make various responses to those scriptural words, and then eat bread and drink wine through which (by God's grace) the Lord of the community is made present to them again. Eucharist, then, is a sacramental ritual in which something—God's presence through Christ— is not simply recalled as past, or pointed to as important, but enacted, made real in the community.

Liturgy

But we still haven't defined *liturgy*. Why do we call the sacramental food ritual of the Eucharist a liturgy? And how is the presence of Christ in that food ritual related to the way we ourselves become Christian?

Among Christian rituals, the Eucharist (or communion, or the Mass, etc.) has a pride of place. While it has been practiced in a variety of ways in different times and places, we have good evidence that this ritual of the Eucharist became very early the principal way in which Christians marked their gatherings weekly—perhaps even daily, in addition to other prayers—in which they understood themselves to be connected again to their Lord, who was risen and ascended but still present to them and empowering them to go out to others with the good news of God's radical forgiveness and unconditional love for the world. Over time, the term *liturgy* came to be used as shorthand for this food ritual. When the term is used broadly, it can refer to any number of rituals that Christians do: burials, daily prayer, ministry to the sick, and so forth. All these liturgies, or rituals, bring to pass the connection to God and related features of Christian identity that they

7

point to. But when the reference is to THE liturgy, in most contexts the reference is specifically to the Eucharist. Why?

In the world in which Christianity emerged—a Greek speaking, Roman and later Byzantine political and cultural environment—a liturgy (*leitourgia*) was an act done by a benefactor for the sake of the people's common life. It was also closely related to religious rituals performed in the temples that benefactors might support. Two senses of the term, then—a (religious) work *of* the people and a work done *for* the good of the public came together in Christian usage. That usage suggests the instinct of Christians that in the Eucharist, two things happen: God is thanked and praised, and the church joins in God's own activity to do something on behalf of the world. God, the one true benefactor of the world, has done a work for the world in Jesus Christ, loving it, saving it, and calling it to communion with God. As Robert Taft has put it, in the deepest sense, the one true *liturgy* is God's work of salvation in Jesus Christ. In the Eucharist, the Christian community joins in that work made present to it again and participates in God's love enacted, made real in the world. The church, in fact, both commits to working together in the great benefaction of God's gift of love through Christ, and is empowered to be part of it. In this way, Christian faith is renewed again and again in the Eucharist, not simply as a set of ideas to be held, but a form of life to be lived.

We can see, then, how the terms ritual, sacrament, and liturgy finally converge on a basic idea for Christians: that through its Eucharistic thanksgiving to God, rendered through the hearing of Scripture and the eating of sacred food, something is not just recalled, but enacted; not just talked about appreciatively but brought to pass again. We don't just express beliefs in a dramatic way in the Eucharist, but we become, like our young man who acted a certain way until he became who he acted, a people of God who are ourselves a continuing part of what God is doing in the world out of love.

Of course, Christians do not do this perfectly, or immediately, or easily, and there are moments in the liturgy when we acknowledge our own failure to enter fully into participation in the one liturgy of God who is Jesus Christ. We will turn to that element, and all the other elements of the liturgy of the Eucharist soon enough. For the moment, it is worth making sure that we have grasped this central point: that the Eucharist is a ritualization, through the eating of sacred food, of an identity into which we ourselves are called by the grace and invitation of the One who has made us and is the deepest end of our desire.

St. Augustine, a great theologian of the Western church, was once reflecting with the newly baptized on the idea in Christian Scriptures that the church is "the Body of Christ." Augustine pointed to the bread and wine on the altar and said to the newly baptized:

> If it's you that are the body of Christ and its members, it's the mystery meaning you that has been placed on the Lord's table. . . . It is to what you are that you reply *Amen*, and by so replying you express your assent. . . . So be a member of the body of Christ, in order to make that *Amen* true. . . . Be what you can see, and receive what you are.[3]

A very similar sentiment is expressed in more contemporary terms by Robert Taft, an Eastern rite Catholic scholar of liturgy. Taft said:

> If the Bible is the Word of God in the words of [human beings], the liturgy is the deeds of God in the actions of those men and women who would live in [God]. . . . The purpose of baptism is to make *us* cleansing waters and healing and strengthening oil; the purpose of Eucharist is not to change bread and wine, but to change you and me: through baptism and eucharist it is *we* who are to become Christ for one another, and a sign to the world that is yet to hear his name. That is what Christian liturgy is all about, because that is what Christianity is all about.[4]

With all this in mind, we turn now to the environment, structure, and texture of the Eucharistic liturgy itself, for the way in which we enact in liturgy both thanksgiving for the love of God and embodiment of the love of God is through the specific prayers, gestures, words, and actions of the rite. In this book, we will focus our reflections about the sacramental liturgy of the Eucharist on the rite—the specific ritual form—that it takes in the 1979 Book of Common Prayer, the authorized liturgical text of the Episcopal Church, and on volume 1 of *Enriching Our Worship*, one of the supplemental liturgical resources that are also authorized for use in the Episcopal Church. The understanding that we seek of the liturgy is aimed, in the end, not at being informed about the liturgy, but being ready to be formed by it, to embody the love of the One who first loved us.

CHAPTER 1

The Sacred Geography of the Liturgy

I f the liturgy involves embodiment of a way of being in the world—grateful, compassionate, relying on God for our life and well-being, etc.—and bodies move in space, then we should include in our explanation of the liturgy a few words about the space in which liturgy occurs. Most rituals either occur in sacred space, or make sacred the space in which they occur, often both. The Eucharistic liturgy typically occurs in a church, a term that really means the people of God (from a Greek term meaning "the Lord's"), but a word we now tend to use for the physical space in which the liturgy is done. Space too, like the liturgy as a whole, enacts what it means to be Christian.

There is a great variety of spaces in which the liturgy occurs. We will not even begin to attempt to describe the differences among the many architectural styles of churches in East or West, but we can say something about the *centers* of the sacred space. Those centers are the key to the sacred geography of the liturgy, even though the centers are themselves arranged in various ways within the room.

The centers of liturgical space are three: the place where the Scriptures are read, the place where new members of the community of faith are initiated, and the place where the community gathers to eat its sacred food. In short, the centers of the sacred geography are the Ambo, the Font, and the Table. The liturgy not only occurs within them but reinforces their significance in the process.

The Ambo is the place from which the Scriptures are read and, perhaps, the sermon is preached. In some churches, particularly those built in recent years, the Ambo is a single lectern, podium, or standing desk; in older churches, there will often be more than one such piece of furniture that serve together as this liturgical center. Perhaps the Scriptures will be read from one and the sermon delivered from the other. Since the hearing of the Word and the preaching of the Word are linked, we will talk about the Ambo here in the singular.

The Ambo stands in the midst of the people, a symbol of Christian life as marked by *responsiveness to God*. We are hearers of the Word, listening in our sacred texts for the Word of God to be spoken: calling, coaxing, commanding, instructing, encouraging, judging, renewing. Some Christians—only a few, historically speaking, and restricted largely to the modern era—take the Bible literally. For most Christians the Bible is the Word of God in human words. Strictly speaking, Jesus alone is the Word of God, in whose life we witness the gracious call to a transformed life of gratitude and care for others, and the forgiveness of sin. Yet it is the Bible that speaks of Jesus as the Word, and so the Bible is the Word of God because it bears witness to that Word who is Jesus Christ, and it reveals God's care and call to us. Christians do not simply direct their own lives and destinies but orient themselves toward God as those who listen, receive, and obey the commands of God as the law of life, the outlines of a life well lived, the path to human flourishing as God intends for us.

The Font is linked to the Word, as in fact all three of the centers are to each other. The Font is the receptacle that holds the water by which new members of the community of God-followers are initiated. Some are small and off to the side, but increasingly churches have returned to an older pattern in which the font is prominent, linked spatially to Word and Table, or perhaps placed by the door as a reminder to all that it is by their baptism that they have been incorporated into the community that knows itself as the very Body of Christ. In baptism, water is poured over the heads or bodies of initiates, and the rich ambiguity of water is key to the ritual. Water cleanses and waters drowns; water washes the earth clean and, in great amounts, destroys; water refreshes, and renews. The ambiguity of water is an appropriate symbol, then, for Christian initiation: those who enter into a life lived before God through Jesus Christ die to an old life and awaken to new life, true life, by God's Word; they are refreshed and renewed and made clean not by their own doing, but by God whose radical love and forgiveness is freely offered to all. Being forgiven and reborn, they commence a life in which they promise to celebrate in gratitude the life they have been given; trust in God; be faithful members of the church that testifies to God's grace by its mission and outreach to the world; care for the dignity of all human beings who are made in God's image; and return again, with the help of God, whenever they fail to keep these promises.

The Table, or Altar, is the place where the community of faith, baptized into this life of responsive trust, gratitude, and compassionate care for God's world is strengthened daily to continue that work by the presence of the risen Lord Jesus, who commanded that his followers share this meal to remember him. At the same time, eating the sacred food, we become what we eat. (Remember Augustine's teaching at the end of the last chapter.) Since the focus of this book is on the Eucharist, a ritual that culminates in this sacred eating, we will have much more to say on this in subsequent sections.

It is worth noticing the theme that unites all three of the centers of Christian liturgy: Word, Font and Table. In each case, and taken together, they signify what we might call life as the *second moment.* Christians are people who aspire to recognize, celebrate, and return repeatedly to the wondrous truth that all life is lived in grateful response to the One from whom life flows. God gives all life, shares the divine being, boundless and mysterious and yet overflowing by God's own good will, into the creation of a world dependent on this first moment in which *God gives all.* God's love and lifegiving Word, of which Jesus Christ is the ultimate sacrament, is the *first moment* of the being of all creatures; God is the One in whom "we live, and move and have our being" (Acts 17:28). All of human life is the *second moment,* in which we hear (think of the Ambo), respond (think of the Font), and are nourished and empowered again (think of the Table) by that which God gives.

CHAPTER 2

The Structure
of the Liturgy

he meaning of liturgy is produced not simply by the words, gestures, ceremonial actions and movement *in* it, but by its structure. The sequence in which we do things liturgically, and the relationships among the liturgy's parts, has a great deal to do with our becoming certain kinds of persons before God.

There is a word used for the most foundational level of the liturgy's structure. It is called the *ordo*. If a sentence can say something only because it follows the grammatical rules of the language in which it is written, so the liturgy—the things we say, do, and sing, and the movements and gestures we make—is possible only as it unfolds by the "rules" of the ordo. In this chapter, we will consider the ordo, or deep grammar, of the liturgy. In fact, we will consider the ordo as something that operates simultaneously at two complementary levels.

The first level at which the ordo operates is a pattern of *proclamation and response*. The liturgy as a whole is composed of two parts, "Word" and "Sacrament," and each of those parts has a central element within it. In the Book of Common Prayer 1979, the liturgical book of the Episcopal Church, the two parts are called "The Word of God" and "The Holy Communion." In its first part, from the beginning of the service to the time at which practitioners share God's peace with one another in an exchange of greetings, we hear the Word of God proclaimed. After gathering and praising God, we sit and listen to the readings of Scripture, and listen to a sermon or homily (another word for sermon). The amount of time involved, as well as the place of the reading and proclamation of the Word within the rite, make this hearing-and-meditating act of attending to Holy Scriptures the centerpiece of this first major part of the liturgy.

The second part of the liturgy, the Sacrament, centers on the communion of the people. This part begins at the offering of bread, wine, and money to support the work to which God calls us, and ends at the dismissal of the people that concludes the whole liturgy. Most of this second part of the liturgy is devoted to communion and the long prayer over the table that precedes it, called the *Eucharistic prayer,* which prepares the bread and wine through the praise of God and petition for the blessing of God's Spirit on the people and the elements of bread and wine that they receive.

So the liturgy of the Word (as the first part is sometimes called) involves the proclamation of God's Word in which we are forgiven, loved, guided, and blessed; and, in response to this proclamation, in the liturgy of the Table (as it is sometimes called), we move to encounter Christ in bread and wine and be empowered to live in the world in a manner befitting this proclamation.

This first of the two levels of the ordo or deep grammar of the liturgy—proclamation and response—does not end with the relationship of the two parts of the liturgy, Word and Sacrament, to each other. When you move from the widest angle of view on the whole liturgy to the elements within each part, like turning a microscope to a higher magnification, you see that the pattern of proclamation and response exists *within* each of the two main parts of the liturgy and not just *between* them. In the first part—again from the beginning of the whole liturgy to the time of the exchange of Peace—we hear the Word of God *proclaimed* in the Scripture and the homiletic reflection on the Scriptures. Then we *respond* by proclaiming our faith in God through the words of an ancient Christian creed, offering prayers for the world and the church, and often confessing the ways we have fallen short of growing into the kind of life God has given us. Within the second part of the liturgy, beginning with the offertory and going to the end, this pattern of proclamation and response is also visible. In the Eucharistic prayer, the whole history of God's saving and loving the world is recounted, *proclaimed*, as an act of thanksgiving for what God has done. In *response* to that proclamation, we receive the bread and wine of the Eucharist that signifies our identity as members of Christ's body who are meant to enflesh and continue his ministry in the world. In fact, if you turn this microscope even further, the Eucharistic prayer itself reflects this pattern of proclamation and response. In the first half of the prayer, God is praised for the history of salvation, and in the second half of the prayer, we respond by calling for God's blessing on the bread and wine, and on us, that we might become the people of God in the world.

By now, one reading this book might be starting to wonder if this twofold pattern of proclamation and response that is the first level of the ordo has anything to do with the twofold first moment and second moment that connects the spatial centers of the Word, Font, and Table together that we explored in the last chapter. In fact, they do. Proclamation precedes response, just as the first moment of God's creation, self-giving, love, and redeeming of the world precedes the second moment of our making baptismal promises and becoming the kind of people who are grateful for God's beneficence, compassionate toward others, and responsible for any hurt that we cause to others and to ourselves.

If the pattern of proclamation and response is the first level of the ordo of the liturgy, found throughout the liturgy like the concentric rings of a tree trunk, there is a second level that complements it. Here we get a little closer to the actual things that are done *in* the rite itself. That second level of the order can be lined out as follow:

- gather in God's name;
- hear and respond to the Word of God;
- pray for the world and the church;
- exchange the Peace with one another;
- prepare the Table;
- give thanks;

- break the bread;
- share the Body and Blood of Christ;
- and be sent forth into the world.

Gathering in God's name begins with praise and thanksgiving, for our gathering is that second moment that responds to the God who first loves us. The Word of God continues the proclamation as we engage with the Scripture as testimony to that first moment. That first moment of God's love is not a moment in time, really, but a continuous initiative of love, of merciful judgment, and of redemption that God does throughout history, manifested fully in the life, death, and resurrection of Jesus Christ. Our prayers for the world and our willingness to make peace with one another both flow from the proclamation of God's call and promise of salvation in the Scripture. So, too, is the preparation and sharing of the table where we encounter again the faithful love of God in Christ who is risen and present with us in our table sharing. All this leads us to go into the world both as witnesses to God's love and as enactors of that love in the wider world.

In the end, the whole pattern of the liturgy's ordo can be mapped like this:

Word		Sacrament
"The Word of God"	||	"Holy Communion"
Proclaim	||	Respond
Gather/Hear&Respond/	||	Prepare/Thank/Break/
Pray/Make Peace		Share/Go Forth
Proclaim Respond	||	Proclaim Respond

Perhaps, too, in the end the entire liturgy is proclamation: the gathering of the people of God is from beginning to end the worship of God from whom all life flows, whose worship inspires and empowers the people of God to respond. The form of that response is to return to the world and engage again, by God's grace and help, in the building of the kingdom that is ultimately God's work.

What remains for us is to explore the elements of the liturgy, the specific things we say and do, which bring this ordo to life.

CHAPTER 3

What We Do in
the Liturgy

I n the next two chapters we will "walk through" the liturgy, offering theological and devotional observations about its elements. For this exploration, we will use The Book of Common Prayer, which contains the authorized texts of the Episcopal Church, along with the first volume of *Enriching Our Worship*, an authorized supplemental resource containing additional materials to be used in the liturgy. The current edition of The Book of Common Prayer was authorized in 1979. There have been many prayer books in the history of the Episcopal Church and in the Church of England from which the Episcopal Church descends. The current prayer book makes a notable shift from those that preceded it, making baptism more central to the life of the community; significantly strengthening the Eucharistic center of the community; and incorporating proper liturgies for the very important days leading up to the celebration of the resurrection (Easter), among other changes. There are two rites for the Eucharist in The Book of Common Prayer. The language of the first is closer to formal vernacular of sixteenth-century English and the latter is in contemporary language. The parts of the liturgy in each rite are roughly parallel, but the second rite reflects a greater breadth of imagery and ideas from the Christian tradition, especially when it comes to the human predicament and the salvation of God directed to our plight, and *Enriching Our Worship* extends the range even more. In addition to being in contemporary language, data suggests that what parishes in the Episcopal Church consider their main Sunday liturgy is overwhelmingly celebrated with Rite II, so we will use that rite for our reflection. For ease, we will refer hereafter to The Book of Common Prayer as the BCP or the prayer book, and *Enriching Our Worship*, volume 1, as EOW1.

The Word of God

The first part of the liturgy, which begins on page 355 of the BCP, is sometimes referred to as the "entrance rite." It includes an opening acclamation, a song of praise, and a prayer or prayers that root the celebration in the praise of God. The entrance rite serves the function of getting the leaders of the liturgy to their places, and preparing the people to hear the Scriptures together. The movement of the liturgy's leaders may be quite elaborate or rather simple. Typically a cross will lead the procession in. In churches that are more elaborately ceremonial (something we call "high church," though that is not what the term used to mean), incense may also be carried in procession and used at other times during the liturgy. As in most religions, the use of incense in Christian practice is a way to set aside the sacred space and make it ready for the momentous action that involves the approach of mortals to the divine presence. In Psalm 141:2, which is used an an opening sentence in the prayer book's service of Evening Prayer (pages 61, 115), incense in linked metaphorically to the "rising" of prayer to God. If incense is used, one or more of the centers of the liturgy may be censed (Word, Font, Table), either during the entrance rite or at points later in the liturgy when those centers will come into play.

The Acclamation. If the liturgy of the people of God is what we have called the second moment—a response to the first moment of God's initiative to give life and to love, to heal and redeem, to call and to save—then it is fitting that the liturgy begins with praise and an acclamation of God. Before another word is spoken, the first words out of

the mouths of a congregation in liturgy are a grateful acknowledgement of God's being and purpose:

> Blessed be God, Father, Son, and Holy Spirit.
>
> People: And blessed be his kingdom, now and forever.
>
> Amen.

This acclamation, which can be replaced by other options from
the BCP and EOW1 that have the same function, sets the tone of a
liturgy named by a Greek term that means "to give thanks." And so
we begin at the beginning, thankfully naming the God in whose name
we gather. This is the purpose for which we were made: to know the
source of our lives and to give thanks for what God has done.

Consistent with this beginning in the acknowledgement and praise
of God, if the liturgy includes music (as it typically does on a Sunday),
it will often begin with a hymn leading into the acclamation and sharing the same purpose. The acclamation itself may be selected to ac-
cord with the seasons of the church year that each focus from a different point of view on the mystery of God made visible in Jesus Christ.
It is worth taking a moment to note the themes of those seasons.

Advent, Christmas, and Epiphany, sometimes called the Incarnation Cycle, run from late in November or early December to around
the second month of the calendar year. Advent focuses on the coming
of Christ and the judgment that awaits us, together with the mercy of
God in Christ whom we trust both to make us ready for that judgment
as we live into the life into which God has called us AND to forgive
where we are unworthy and fall short. Christmas celebrates the incarnation of God in Jesus the Word—the love of God made visible and
concrete in a world of finite, limited, and mortal things. Through the
Incarnation, the paradox of God's presence in the world is revealed:
that the One from whom all beings draw their very existence would
be present in one very form in which that existence takes shape. This
is the length to which God will go to bring in the reign of God in the
world. Epiphany, especially in the Western church, focuses on the gift
of God through Jesus the Jew to the Gentiles, that is, to the people of

the whole world, and inspires our response to the Word he preached in the form of our own mission and ministry to all God's people.

The Paschal Cycle (from a Greek term that translates the Hebrew for "Passover") includes Lent, Easter (a season, not just a day), and Pentecost, the conclusion of the Easter season. The timing of the end of Epiphany and beginning of Lent is determined by when the movable feast of Easter falls. Lent is a time to simplify, refocus one's priorities so that the desire for God is uppermost and reflected in our actions, and accept responsibility for the sins we commit against God, others, and ourselves. Easter begins with the Feast of the Resurrection of Jesus, whose Incarnation of God's love was more powerful than the grave into which he was placed by our resistance to his life and ministry. The life, death, and resurrection of Christ constitute a symphony of fierce love that finds its crescendo in Holy Week and Easter. Using special liturgies that lead to Easter Day—found in the Book of Common Prayer on pages 270 through 295—Christians linger and wonder over the power of God that arises from death and is not overcome by it. Pentecost concludes the Easter season, generally around very early June, with a celebration of God's continuing presence to us through the Spirit. Following Pentecost comes a long season of focus on the implications of the church's practice of the kingdom of God in the world, and the entire liturgical year begins again.

There is much more to say about the calendar, and about the special liturgies of Maundy Thursday, Good Friday, and the Great Vigil of Easter that form the center of the Christian year, but they are beyond our scope here. We will satisfy ourselves with one other observation: that the Scripture readings for Sundays, on which Christians regather again to give thanks to God and to ritually enact their identity as members of the kingdom of God, are tied to the theme and rhythm of the calendar and change on a three-year cycle known as a *lectionary*. The lectionary included in the Book of Common Prayer, which as an exception can still be used by parishes not ready to make a transition, has been replaced by The Revised Common Lectionary, an ecumenical project that improves on the prayer book lectionary by including significant portions of Scripture not previously included in western lectionaries. It also includes an option for readings from the Old Testament in sequence, rather than by thematic selection. A person who participates in the liturgy of the Episcopal Church each Sunday for three years hears an enormous amount of the Bible read and pondered.

Returning to our walk through the liturgy . . .

The Song of Praise. After an optional prayer asking God to make us worthy to worship, the liturgy continues with a song of praise that can be replaced, during certain seasons, with a song of prayer for God's mercy. The hymn of praise known as the *Gloria* (often a hymn is named for its first word or words in Latin, the language that dominated Western Christianity for many centuries) begins with words taken directly from the section of Scripture in which the birth of Jesus is proclaimed. The rest of the Gloria developed in the early centuries of the church as a hymn for use in the liturgy. This use of scriptural language is not unusual in the liturgy: not only is Scripture read and proclaimed, but it often forms the very words in which praises and prayers are offered or grounded. The rubrics of the prayer book (a term for the rules that sometimes prescribe, sometimes indicate options for the way the rite is performed) indicate that the Gloria is used as the normal hymn of praise on Sundays from Christmas Day through Epiphany (January 6); from Easter through Pentecost; and on the days of Easter Week and Ascension Day; and at other times as desired. This ebullient form of praise is not used in Advent or Lent, whose themes of preparation and thoughtful inventory of the ways in which our lives do not yet reflect the light of God lend themselves to more reflective forms.

There are times when our praise of God is appropriately coupled with a plea for mercy, especially in seasons when we are reflecting on the ways in which we fall short of embodying the life and love of the kingdom of God. At such times, and on other occasions as desired, the ancient hymns of the *Trisagion* or *Kyrie* (taken, in this case, from the Greek for "three-times holy," and "Lord," respectively) will be offered instead of the Gloria. Yet even our plea for the mercy of God is couched in the language of acclamation: the Kyrie descends from a form of acclamation of the emperor, and in the Trisagion, too, the request for God's mercy follows out from the naming of God:

Holy God,
Holy and Mighty,
Holy Immortal One,
Have mercy on us.

*The Collect.*As we approach the moment to hear the Scriptures, a prayer for the day is offered in a form known as a *Collect*. (This is pronounced *Coll*-ect, with the emphasis on the first syllable.) Though there are some recent exceptions in EOW1, a collect normally begins in the first part with the naming of God by some attribute or action:

Almighty God, you have poured upon us the new light
of your incarnate Word. . . .

And, after attributing these characteristics to God, offers a petition for God in the second part that God might do something in our own time and circumstance, consistent with the attributes of the first part.

Grant that this light, enkindled in our hearts,
may show forth in our lives. . . .

These excerpts come from the Collect for the First Sunday after Christmas Day. There is a different collect for each Sunday and a number of other occasions, and with a few exceptions, the collect is linked with the themes of the day and season and with the Scripture lessons appointed for the day. The prayer book's calendar can be found on pages 15 through 33 of the prayer book, and the appointed lessons, or "propers," at the very end of the book.

Most of the entrance rite is sung or said standing, though in some congregations or during some seasons, the Collect of the Day may be said kneeling.

After we have offered our praise and worship, honoring that first moment of the glory of God's being and God's goodness toward us, and after we have prayed for God to grant to us what we need to walk the path of the kingdom, we are ready to hear the reading of the Scriptures.

The Lessons and Sermon. The Bible for Christians, as noted earlier, is the Word of God in the words of human beings. Testifying ultimately to the living Word of Jesus Christ, the Christian Bible is a version of the Jewish Scriptures, plus four of the ancient gospels of the Christian Church (narratives of Jesus' life, death, resurrection, and postresurrection appearances and commands), the letters of Paul, John, and other unnamed early Christian writers, and other materials. Episcopalians also read the Apocrypha: texts that, while not quite holding the status of sacred Scripture, have often been read for the instruction and upbuilding of the church.

Christians read the Bible not simply as an artifact of the belief or practice of earlier times, though it certainly is that; nor as a literal instruction book or blueprint for our every decision, though there are certainly commands and exhortations in the Bible; but rather as the story of the faith of a community, and the long narrative of God's manner of salvation. A book full of diverse texts—from history, law, and narrative, to parables and instruction, hymns and wisdom literature—the Bible reads us as much as we read it. It names the human condition in all its glory, brokenness, depravity, and capability, and names God's orientation to us in all those aspects: God is *for* us, creating us to be in communion with God and one another and constantly provoking, calling, and strengthening us to live into that purpose. It does so through a staggering diversity and range of material that testifies to human wandering and waywardness, as well as fidelity and harmony. The charge of the Bible, given the moments of human infidelity and obstinacy, is to inhabit the world again in harmony with all creation and with one another—the charge conveyed notionally in the book of Genesis and celebrated in the Jewish notion of *tikkun o'lam*—roughly, the healing or mending of the world. For Christians, the beginning and the end of the world's order and healing is found in the life, death, and resurrection of Jesus Christ, and so we read the

Bible as whole to be consistent with what we understand is revealed in Jesus Christ.

This is sometimes a tall order to read the Bible in this way. Respect for the Bible involves an understanding of what each book is about in its context, so that it can speak to us in ours. Further, the Scriptures offer a very unvarnished view of the habits and inclinations of human nature. Yet at each reading of the Old and New Testament lessons, we say, "The Word of the Lord." Although particular passages may not always be flattering to hear, easy to digest, or directly relevant to the culture or knowledge of our day, still we trust that God speaks to us and calls us through them. Provoking, soothing, mourning, calling, praising, and protesting: we listen to the sacred Scriptures from the depth of our being in order to hear God's Word to us, and to be inspired to speak our own words of proclamation, provocation, and comfort to the world in God's name.

The prayer book prescribes up to three lessons from Scripture to be read. Ceremonially, there are two common ways in which this occurs. In one approach, the lessons from the Old and New Testaments will be read from the Ambo (or lectern) and the lessons from the Gospel read from a separate book, often beautifully adorned. This way of separating out the gospels cements through ritual the notion that Jesus, for Christians, is the clue to the whole Bible and that the gospels are the lens through which the whole Bible is read. Thus, the gospels have a place of honor in the ritual manner in which we read them. In recent years, with a concern to honor the Jewishness of Jesus and the story of Israel that is the textual and spiritual foundation of the Christian gospel, the gospel may be read from the large Bible that sits on the Ambo, signaling its unity with the whole of Scripture's testimony to the fierce fidelity and steadfast love of God, flowing forth out of the history of the people Israel, not to displace them as the covenant people, but to embrace the world.

Among the readings a psalm is appointed. The psalms of the Hebrew Bible are songs, and often express the rawest of human emotions: from deep, transforming confidence in God to feelings of being abandoned and alone; from outrage at enemies to pleas for the help of God in the face of the derision and mockery of others; from tender devotion to contrition for sin; and more. The psalms are blunt and honest, and their inclusion in our worship counters the popular notion in some Christian circles that God cannot be questioned or challenged, that it would be irreverent to call God on the carpet for seeming not to help in time of trouble, or to challenge God for being hidden in time of need. To the contrary: Christian faith arises as an offshoot of the faith of Israel, Christians depending on the grace of God to be grafted onto that heritage of those who remain the people of God, according to St. Paul. In the Hebrew Scriptures, Abraham argued with God about the threshold of sin over which he would destroy Sodom for its violation of hospitality. Job challenged God for the evils that befell him, in spite of Job's righteousness and fidelity. Jesus the Jew cried out in frustration and desolation on the cross, wondering why God had forsaken him. In the twentieth century, the Jews of Auschwitz put God on trial for failing to keep the covenant. This is not a tradition in which one must fear honest expression of feelings before God. The name *Israel* means, roughly, "to struggle with God." Pietistic refusals among Christians to speak honestly to God, even to challenge and question God when that arises naturally from difficult times, have forgotten their heritage and the desire of God to be in relationship with God's creatures. The psalms are one moment, though not the only moment, in the readings of Scripture when humans dare, even within the framework of praise and thanksgiving, to lay their confusion, mourning, lamentation, and questions before God's throne. God does not want automatons to worship; God desires relationship, and relationship requires honesty.

After the readings, the prayer book prescribes a sermon. The sermon is the Christian version of a long practice, rooted in Judaism, of finding in the Scripture a dialogue partner in the process of living a human life well. The Scripture has pride of place in this dialogue, but the Scripture does not self-interpret. This is the problem with literal interpretation of the Scripture from an Anglican point of view, and Episcopalians do not generally read the Scripture literally. Rather, we read the Scripture and engage with it, so that the living Word of God may speak freshly to our situation and struggles. The preacher does not so much tell the people how to understand the Scriptures, but engage in a dialogue with it both "in front of them" and as one of them, modeling and inviting us all into the same engagement.

The Creed. At this point in the liturgy, the assembly takes a turn in its ritual work. Remember all that we have discovered about the pattern of proclamation and response discussed in the earlier chapters. So when the Word of God has been proclaimed through the reading and preaching of Scripture, the people now move into response mode, one that anticipates the further response they will make by moving to the table to commune with God.

The Creed (from the Latin *Credo*) is a statement of belief. There is a great range of theological diversity among Christians, contrary to popular conceptions (especially in America). The Scriptures themselves represent an almost dizzying array of diverse concepts, metaphors, and discourse about God, arising from the culturally and historically diverse settings in which the various texts were written. The history of Christianity, too, shows dynamic growth and development over time. Christians are not bound together by doctrinal agreement, even though some Christian groups place a very high value on this. The claim that doctrinal agreement is what holds us together is simply not historically supportable. Christians are bound together by their commitment to a person: Jesus Christ, mysteriously divine and human, in whom God reveals the ultimate purpose and meaning of life in creation.

Even with the diversity of Christianity, there are certain theological watersheds in the history of Christian belief and, for the Eastern and Western churches, the Nicene Creed is one of those watersheds. The creed was produced in the fourth century at the ecumenical councils of Nicea and Constantinople. What the creed represents is a kind of fundamental affirmation that the work of the Jesus, the creator God, and the Spirit are the work of one God, three in one; and that Jesus is at one and the same time divine and human, the very incarnation of the divine *logos*, or divine reason, by which the

28

whole world is structured and animated. (Jesus' humanity and divinity is further elaborated in the creed of Chalcedon, found in a group of historical documents included on page 864 of the prayer book.) The need to sort this out arose out of the tension created when followers of Jesus, rooted in a tradition in which God is one, and is not visible in any form within the creation, at the same time found themselves so moved by Jesus Christ that they could not deny God was somehow "in him" in a singular way. The Nicene Creed attempts to resolve this tension in language drawn from the Greek philosophical milieu in which Christians lived that could affirm both their monotheistic roots and their confidence in the divine identity of Jesus. This creedal claim about the Trinity and the divine-human identity of Jesus that Christians make is a mystery, not in the sense that we have a question about it, but in the ancient Greek sense of mystery: something that we know truly by faith, and can articulate by some measure of reason, but which is deeper than reason can reach. By the measure of this creed, the range of diverse ways in which Christians think and speak about Jesus are all legitimate so long as they deny neither his being the embodiment of the divine nor his being fully and completely human.

Not all Christians around the world are committed to the Nicene Creed. Some, Christians, particularly in the churches of the Middle East, have different ways of articulating the relationship between God and Jesus and the human and divine in Jesus, and even Eastern and Western Christians differ profoundly over a particular clause in the creed that we say differently; but, again, all Christians remain bound together by their commitment that in Jesus God's own self was at work in a way that has universal saving significance for people of all times and places. The Creed IS the way that Western Christians articulate this Trinitarian mystery and so it becomes the first act in a responsive arc that the liturgical assembly makes after it hears the Word.

The affirmation is framed in the language of Christians deeply rooted in an intellectual culture of neo-Platonism, and is in some ways foreign to our intellectual modes today. But those who study ritual would say that there is something more going on at the moment when the people say the Creed than simply an affirmation of the content. Crucially, it comes immediately after we have heard the Scriptures read and preached, that we stand—rousing ourselves in response to what we have heard—and speak in one voice together. Ritually, standing creates a formality and a communal sense of identity that is not as pronounced when we sit or kneel, and so, not only the response that *is* the Creed, but the necessary act of a resounding response *itself* is signaled at this point when we rise to our feet. The Word of God has been proclaimed; Christians are roused at this moment to reaffirm the faith that the Scriptures have deepened and fortified, and do so in a language that signifies their place in the tradition of their forebears who also tried, by grace and best effort, to follow the way of Jesus Christ.

Prayers of the People. If Christian life is a life of hearing, of listening and responding to God's call, ritually enacted in the liturgy in the ways we have seen so far, then there is no more fitting response to the God who self-offers in the gift of Jesus Christ to the world than to offer intercessory prayers. Jesus himself, in terms that made sense in the Jewish world of his day when the second temple still stood in Jerusalem, is presented in the Scriptures, among other ways, as our high priest. Before going to the cross, in the gospel of John, he offers what scholars call a "high priestly prayer" for those around him; and in the book of Hebrews, the metaphor of Jesus as our high priest is a powerful way to present Jesus as one who goes before God on our behalf. If, through the Eucharist, Christians are to become the Body of Christ (as St. Paul, St. Augustine, Robert Taft, and so many others put it), then the priestly character of Christ, standing before God with the great need of the world to be healed and saved, is an important part of being Christian as well. Early on, we said that the liturgy was as much about becoming certain kinds of people as about believing certain things: in the Prayers of the People, we both offer intercessions for those in need and become the kind of people whose work is to offer intercession.

The intercessions may be offered in a number of ways. They can be bidden by the deacon and then offered by a layperson; they may be led from the midst of the congregation or read from the Ambo. The presider (the 1979 BCP calls her or him the "celebrant") always gathers up the intercessions and concludes them in a final prayer to God. The BCP provides six models for intercession that are often used—some would now say too often—and the better practice, increasingly done, is for congregations to develop their own ways to offer intercession in their own idiom and sensitive to their own context. What the BCP prescribes (p. 383) is simply that intercessions always be made for:

The Universal Church
The Nation and all in authority
The welfare of the world
The concerns of the local community
Those who suffer and those in any trouble
Those who have died.

The privilege of entering into the saving work of Christ by praying for others is a mystery. Philosophers and theologians have long pondered the tangles and knots of thinking involved in the offering of prayers to the divine. If God is divine, does God not know what is needed and therefore not require prayer? Does prayer change God's mind or bring something to God's attention previously inaccessible to divine knowledge? Can God change? In the Hebrew Scriptures, different than in the Greek philosophical worldview we have so much inherited, God is presented as everlasting, but not unchanging.[5] Perhaps God does truly change in response to human requests? Whatever one makes of this conundrum, we are bidden, repeatedly and consistently throughout Scripture, to pray. While the host of questions about prayer are worthy of reflection, perhaps we can simply say here that, along the lines of Taft's interpretation of baptismal waters and Eucharistic food, the point of intercessory prayer is not so much to change God or direct God to something God does not know, but to change us: to make us people who, after prayer for those who suffer and struggle, go out into the world to be God's answer to our prayer, caring for the sick and suffering, supporting those in leadership, and entering into *tikkun o'lam*, the healing of the world, in God's name.

The Confession. Neither our work in God's name nor our priestly identity exempts us from the bad choices and missed opportunities to do good that accompany the finitude of human nature. We may seek the mending of the world, but the world is not mended yet, and we are part of what's broken, even as we aspire to enter into the kingdom of God whose outlines we sketch in our ritual action in liturgy. One of the marvelous moments of the liturgy is that it folds into the very framework of ritual actions in which we undertake to enact ourselves as a people grateful for God, attentive to God's Word, and willing to join our lives to the priesthood of Jesus Christ in care for the world, a moment in which we express awareness of our failure to be any of those things very well, and sorrow for failing to do so. Lest one consider the liturgy a kind of idealistic exercise, the Confession joins the psalms and other readings of lamentation that come up in the lectionary in the inclusion of clear-eyed honesty and contrition for our failure to live into the very kingdom life toward which the liturgy moves us.

Confession in the Eucharist is a corporate matter. We are a community, and we make confession as a community for failing to be the Body of Christ before God and in the world. A moment of silence can precede the Confession (BCP p. 360), but it is important to understand that, while this provides a moment in which we might recall some of our own sins before joining others in the words of the Confession, the point is to recognize that our sins contribute, together, to a failure of the church to do its work in joyful obedience to God. In other words, the Confession is not an aggregation of individuals expressing their sorrow for their individual failures at the same time, but a body of people expressing their sorrow for the church's failures to live up to its calling. There are times when personal sins weigh heavily on us, and there is a rite in the BCP for those individuals who wish for help in releasing those sins and accepting God's forgiveness and empowerment to live differently. (See BCP pp. 446–452). The

Confession is an act of the Church, expressing its failure to be itself a sacrament of the kingdom of God in the world and a renewal of its commitment, by God's grace, to do so. Absolution is pronounced by the priest after we have confessed. The priest absolves not as a person with special power but as a sacramental person, a person-as-sign within the community of God's call and presence to them. It is God who forgives, and we—priest and people together—who return to the mending of the world in God's name, knowing we will fail again and sometimes succeed, and that God stands always ready to receive and renew our repentant hearts.

As important as Confession is, there are times when Confession may be omitted in the liturgical year. The refusal to accept that God forgives even before we ask—like the father in the gospel of Luke who comes running to his prodigal son when the son is still far off and has not yet asked for forgiveness—is a sin of its own kind, a kind of pride and excessive valuation of the significance of our failings. There are times in the year when we simply bask in the light of God's acceptance of us. By very long tradition, the Easter season is one of those times, when the celebration of the resurrection of Christ that signifies God's grace and forgiveness extends for fifty days—roughly a seventh of the year. The Easter season is the year's Sabbath, just as Sunday is the week's Sabbath, and the exultation of Christians at their forgiveness resoundingly granted by God makes Confession rather redundant during that season.

The Peace. Again, liturgy produces meaning in large part by its structure. There is a reason why the Peace comes normally at this point in the liturgy: peace comes in being a person who is grateful to God and who knows that one's life is lived under the divine horizon (entrance rite); who hears the Word and seeks to live in communion with God and neighbor (the hearing and pondering of Scripture); who reaches out in compassion toward one's neighbors (intercessions); and who acknowledges dependence on God for forgiveness and renewal (confession). Only after we have ritually enacted those qualities for the sake of living them in all of life are we ready ritually to enact peacemaking with one another—a quality utterly consistent with that aspiration to mend the world, and which we also seek to embody in the world beyond the liturgy.

The Peace is not a social time, but a liturgical action. It is inappropriate to catch up on news, or enter into lengthy conversation about matters that can wait until after the liturgy. In this ritualized exchange, by greeting one another with a handshake, a brief hug, a kiss, and saying "Peace," "the Peace of God," or the like, we signify both that peace is made among us through the proclamation of God's word and that we make peace with one another in grateful response to that Word. The alternative placement of the Peace in the rite is just before communion and has the same ritual effect of response to the proclamation of the story of God's salvation of the world.

Being at peace before God and one another, we are ready to move to the table rite in which God's presence will be enacted in the grateful consumption of sacred food.

The Holy Communion

We have been focusing on the pattern of proclamation and response as we've moved through the first part of the liturgy. The entire pattern of proclamation and response is grounded and made possible by the fundamental proclamation by God of the Living Word, whose glory and worthiness we signal by the liturgy's first words of acclamation and praise. The form of the *response*—attentive hearing in the context of our struggles, faithful affirmation of confidence in God, compassionate intercession for the world, and honest self-appraisal and recommitment—is ritually enacted after the reading and preaching of Scripture. All this is both the practice and the promise of our participation in the mending of the world that is, most deeply, God's own liturgy through Jesus Christ.

We are far enough along, at this point, to see that this recalls the second dimension of the deep grammar or ordo of the liturgy. The twofold pattern of proclamation and response is carried out through the ninefold pattern of gathering, hearing the Word read and preached.

praying for the world and the church, exchanging the Peace, preparing the table, giving thanks, breaking the bread, sharing the gifts, and going forth into the world. So far we have worked through four of those elements of the liturgy.

Now we prepare the table for the sacred eating through which the presence of God is conveyed to us. It is worth pausing for a moment to remind ourselves of the nature of this sacramental practice and to set it in relationship to Jesus Christ. Christians are rooted firmly in the tradition of Genesis in which God pronounces the created order good. Despite periods in history and particular historical figures who mistakenly have adopted negative attitudes toward the body and the materiality of creation, Christians celebrate the material order as good. God meets us in the physical world and Christians understand God's own creative Word to have been enfleshed in Jesus of Nazareth. As we encounter God through the good world that God has spoken into being by the Spirit, and in the Incarnate Word of God that is Jesus Christ, so too we encounter God in the elements of creation that are part of the warp and woof of our daily lives, like food and the fellowship created around our eating together. Bread and wine, taken in hand by Jesus at his final meal with his disciples (a meal identified by three of the gospels as a Jewish Passover meal), become by his Word and Spirit the sacrament of his continuing presence to us. Recall here our earlier discussion of sacraments as material elements that in the manner of mystery *communicate* and *participate* in that to which they *point*. We understand Christ to be truly present to us in the eating of bread and wine that, by God's grace and through prayer, convey that presence to us.

The Offertory. For ordinary food and wine to become sacramental, we set them in the context of ritual praise and prayer. When we prepare the table for this sacramental celebration, we are offering not only bread and wine, but ourselves, inspired and renewed by the Word of God earlier in the liturgy.

There is no single way in which the table must be prepared for the Eucharist. In most churches on Sundays, though, bread and wine will be brought forward as gifts from the people to signify their own self-offering to God, having been renewed by the proclamation of the Word. Often this is the moment when people will present monetary offerings as well, to go toward the continuing work of the church as the Body of Christ in the world. The significance of this self-offering will often be highlighted ritually by special offerings of music by the choir and, typically, some sort of singing by the people, usually standing, to mark the moment. To be ourselves transformed into the Body and Blood of Christ by receiving the Body and Blood of Christ—as Taft put it, "to become Christ for one another, and a sign to the world that is yet to hear his name"—we first offer ourselves for that transformation through the offertory. That self-offering to God is grounded and inspired by God's own self-offering to us through Jesus, and so our self-offering begins and ends in God. We bring nothing that God has not first given, and our offering is fundamentally one of gratitude and praise.

It is the work of the deacon to set the table for the sacramental feast. Each of the orders of ministry embody something central to the work of the church: bishops overseeing and taking responsibility for the church, priests extending the oversight of the bishop in caring for the world by strengthening and upbuilding the people of God, and deacons serving and drawing the attention of the church to those in need. These are, in fact, the tasks of the whole people with respect to the world: overseeing the world in the sense of responsibility for its leadership and well-being; preaching and sacramentalizing the gospel of salvation and love for all people and standing before God with the world held in the heart; and serving the world, with particular attention to those who suffer. In the liturgy, women and men who have been ordained to these roles perform parts of the liturgy that manifest these tasks to which the whole church is called, clergy and laity together, and they do so as members of the baptized community that shares that work together. To put it another way, the ordained leaders of church are walking, breathing mirrors to the people of God of the work for the sake of the whole creation that belongs, first and foremost, to us all.

The preference expressed by prayer book rubrics is that the people stand for the offertory and Great Thanksgiving, although kneeling during the latter is also permitted and not uncommon. A recovery in this prayer book of an older practice of the church, there is something powerful about the whole assembly standing for this part of the liturgy. The posture of the body is open, celebratory, and communal, cementing the experience of the assembly not as individuals awaiting the benefits of the sacrament for each, but as an irreducibly corporate body engaged in worship, just as the assembly is then a body, not an aggregation of individuals, sent into the world in witness to the kingdom of God.

The Great Thanksgiving. The word *Eucharist*, as noted earlier, means "thanksgiving," and it is through The Great Thanksgiving (more or less synonymous for our purposes with the "Eucharistic prayer") that we offer ourselves to God and that these elements of bread and wine become for us the sacrament of the Body and Blood of Christ. The Great Thanksgiving has a particular structure that, not surprisingly, is consistent with the deep pattern of proclamation and response that we have seen throughout the liturgy already. That pattern, furthermore, is rooted in the pattern of prayer typical of the people of Israel onto whom, according to St. Paul, we have been grafted by God's gracious hospitality. It is worth spending a moment on that pattern.

While there are exceptions, quite frequently formal Jewish prayer is offered with a kind of three-part movement: the acknowledgement of God, the remembrance of what God has done for them, and petition for what is needed from God in the present moment. Even God's own "speech" to the people of Israel often begins with a reminder of what God has done, followed by comfort, exhortation, judgment, or command. The Ten Commandments, the core of the Jewish Torah (law) begins with God's self-identification before commands are made, and both the Torah and the prophets not infrequently return to a reminder that God is the One who brought the people out of the land of Egypt. Only after that shorthand reminder of salvation history does God then offer hope, judgment, consolation, or command. The

Jewish prayer pattern and God's own "speech" to human beings are linked in this way.

This Jewish "logic" of communication between God and God's people, whether in God's Word to the Israelites or their prayer to God, is compressed into two parts and reflected in the Great Thanksgiving. The first part expresses thanks to God for the history of our salvation and only then, after acknowledgement of God and God's work among us, does the second part petition God to bless, by the Spirit, the gifts of bread and wine and the people assembled at the table. Notice how this pattern in the Eucharistic prayer parallels the instinct embedded in the entrance rite at the beginning of the liturgy: acclamation and praise of God come first, and only then does the Collect of the Day offer petition; and the Collect itself begins by naming something of God's attributes or actions, and only then asks for God's response.

One of the distinctive features of the 1979 BCP is that, unlike the American prayer books that preceded it or the English prayer books before them, it has many different options for the Eucharistic prayer. Some Eucharistic prayers (like BCP Prayer A) focus almost entirely on human sin and on the death of Jesus as his sacrifice; others (like EOW Prayer 2) expand sacrifice to apply to Jesus' life, so that the cross becomes the culmination and crown of a whole way of living. Some prayers focus on Wisdom and its link to the creative activity of God (like EOW Prayer 3). Others (like BCP Prayer C) use language appropriate to the sensibility of a people whose technology has allowed for travel to the moon. The choice of which Eucharistic prayer to use is, in most churches, dependent upon local judgment about the themes of the liturgical season we discussed earlier in this book. For example, Prayer B in the BCP or Prayer 2 in EOW1, which highlight Incarnation and the role of Mary, might be used for Advent, Christmas, and Epiphany; or Prayer C in the BCP or Prayer 1 in EOW1, which have particularly strong imagery around sin and brokenness, might be appropriate for Sundays in Lent.

Given the number of Eucharistic prayers—four in Rite II of the BCP, and three more in EOW1—we will consider the structure of the Eucharistic prayer by considering Prayer D as our general model. (BCP p. 372) This is perhaps the fullest and most robust of Eucharistic prayers in the BCP, modeled closely on a prayer from around the fourth century in origin and shared in similar versions by Christians of other traditions. Notwithstanding a few variations from one Eucharistic prayer to the next, this one will provide a good sense of the structure and meaning of this part of the liturgy.

Sursum Corda. The Great Thanksgiving begins with an exchange of greeting between presider and people. This reestablishes the relationship between them as one in which all are involved in the liturgy, and the presider, far from doing things "for" the assembly is, for the sake of the order and movement of the liturgy, leading the people from among them.

Pre-Sanctus. The first part of Prayer D, following our pattern of thanks and acclamation before petition, proclaims God as the mystery of Being itself beyond beings, the source of light and goodness and blessing for all creatures, who created us to rejoice in God as our primary purpose. That first part of any Eucharistic prayer most often focuses on the power and wonder of God the Creator, the first person of the God who is affirmed in the Creed as mysteriously Three in One. Notice that nothing is asked of God in this portion of the prayer. We are in the first part of the prayer in which, consistent with the Jewish pattern, our concern is simply to acknowledge and affirm the reality and power of God. In prayer D, our affirmation of the splendor for God's being is joined to the praise of the angels themselves in a hymn we call the Sanctus, by the first word of the text in Latin, which means "Holy."

Sanctus. The holiness of God is a strong theme in the Old Testament, present here in the Sanctus, which echoes the words of the high angels in the prophet Isaiah's vision of the dwelling place of God: "Holy, Holy Lord, God of power and might; heaven and earth are full of your glory." God's holiness is God's radical otherness from the created order, sacred and separate and beyond the approach of finite creatures, all purity and power and being itself. The proper response to the holiness of God is to cover one's face, to fall on the ground before the One, as Prayer D has just put it, who dwells "in light inaccessible from before time and forever." And yet . . .

Benedictus. Our worshipful cry, "Holy, Holy, Holy," is coupled with the acclamation, "Blessed is he who comes in the name of the Lord. Hosanna in the highest." The Benedictus too comes directly from Scripture as the acclamation that disciples uttered as Jesus entered Jerusalem. The message communicated by the combination of these two lines is close to the heart of the Christian gospel: the one, holy, living God, who lies beyond all human comprehension and human worthiness to approach, yet makes our approach possible by coming toward us. This is the good news of the gospel of Jesus Christ.

The Sanctus/Benedictus is one of those portions of the liturgy that is sung as a hymn to one of many beautiful settings, some historical, some contemporary. It is usually sung by the whole assembly but, in more elaborate forms, may be offered on behalf of the community by the choir.

Post-Sanctus. In the second major section of the Eucharistic prayer, the focus shifts to praise of God for the long arc of salvation history. Again, we do not approach the Lord with petition but simply with grateful remembrance of all that God has done. The call of God through the people of Israel, who are sometimes named and always implied, leads up to our remembrance that in God's time the Word became flesh in Jesus. In fulsome prayers like Prayer D, the details of Jesus' ministry are celebrated. ("To the poor he proclaimed the good news of salvation; to prisoners, freedom; to the sorrowful, joy.") To include those details of Jesus' life has been a trend in recent Eucharistic prayers, avoiding a narrow model of salvation as the satisfaction of God through the violent death of an innocent and attending instead to Jesus' death as the extent to which Jesus would go with a whole life of self-giving, compassionate love for those broken by sin or cut off by the scapegoating power structures of religious or political institutions. This section often concludes with the recollection of Jesus' death, or death and resurrection as in Prayer D, and turns to the remembrance of the Last Supper. This section, carrying through to the Words of Institution, comes to center on Jesus, thus highlighting the work of the triune God in the second person.

Words of Institution. In all our Eucharistic prayers, we remember the words that Jesus said over the bread and wine in the meal he shared with his disciples just before his death. The words are a kind of summary, since these words are recorded somewhat differently between the gospels of Mark and Matthew, on the one hand, and the gospel of Luke and the letter of St. Paul to the Corinthians, on the other. The importance of the words of Jesus in the prayer is twofold. First, our Eucharistic prayer has been working its way down through history to the fullness of God's gift of salvation made manifest to us in Jesus, so this moment becomes the narrowest and most intimate point of that recollection. We are, in a certain way, at the table with Jesus at this moment, hearing again his command to remember him in this way. Second, at the same time, the Eucharistic prayer is not simply a repetition of the Last Supper, though it is sometimes misunderstood in this way. For the meal we share is a special form of Jesus' presence in which he is with us under the sign of absence, unlike his celebration of the Passover meal with his disciples when he was present in body. We experience Jesus *resurrected*, not as the first disciples did, but as a presence-in-absence in communion with him until the end of time when he returns. In a certain way, the absence of Jesus is important to his presence in us, the assembly. Jesus must "ascend" to God, making space for the community to continue his work in the assurance of its accomplishment and being freed from the limitations of space and time so that he is present in all places and times as God's Living Word has, in fact, always been. The hope of Jesus' return, which Christians understand in many ways, means to affirm that the work of God, begun in Jesus, was both completed in him and yet awaits the full unfolding of the kingdom of God. Christians, empowered by God, participate in and witness to that unfolding. The recitation of the words of Jesus in the Eucharist links our prayer both to his earthly ministry at a single place and time and to the purpose of all history: the mending of the world and its union with its creator.

Anamnesis and Oblation. So this recitation of Jesus' words is not simply nostalgia for the past nor a dramatic reenactment of Jesus' last supper but a remembrance of him in the context of *this* supper, when Christians know him, by faith, in the bread and wine of the Eucharist as One who calls us to continue, by our participation in his work, the unfolding of the kingdom of God. That special kind of remembrance we do in the Eucharist is *anamnesis.* Again, linked to certain forms of Jewish memory and prayer, anamnesis is a way of making the past present, of opening oneself to its impact at this moment. It is not a simple or unmediated presence, in our control, but, as noted above, the presence of the Risen One, drawing us into the future kingdom. In a Eucharistic prayer, the anamnesis and oblation (a term that means offering) is the moment when we draw together all that we have done so far—praising God, recalling salvation history, and speaking again the words of Jesus as the penultimate moment in that history that culminates in Jesus' death and resurrection—and, with the continuing power of that work in our lives, offer the bread and wine for God's blessing. Notice this way in which the anamnesis coordinates with the pattern of proclamation and response that we have seen so frequently already. By implication, in our oblation, we are offering not only the bread and wine for blessing but ourselves as well; as Augustine put it, it is the very mystery of our own identity as the Body of Christ by which we are fed in the sacramental signs of Jesus' presence.

The words in which the anamnesis is made and the oblation promised vary from one Eucharistic prayer to the next, but their logic is generally, "remembering, we offer." In prayer D, the anamnesis and oblation is rendered like this:

> Father, we now celebrate this memorial of our redemption. Recalling Christ's death and his descent among the dead, proclaiming his resurrection and ascension to your right hand, awaiting his coming

in glory; and offering to you, from the gifts you have given us, this bread and this cup, we praise you and we bless you.

Acclamation. In some prayers, and in differing places, the people join together with the presider to voice their praise of God. In Prayer D, the acclamation follows after the anamnesis and oblation, which in turn is followed by the final section of the prayer, in many ways its crescendo.

Epiclesis. Now, and only now, after praise and proclamation, are we ready to make petition. The epiclesis is the point at which the church, through the voice of the presider, asks God to make holy both the gifts of bread and wine and the people who stand around the Table in worship. The center of gravity in the epiclesis will usually be a strong verb like "sanctify," "make," "bless," or the like. Here is the epiclesis and surrounding text from Prayer D:

> Lord, we pray that in your goodness and mercy your Holy Spirit may descend upon us, and upon these gifts, sanctifying them and showing them to be holy gifts for your holy people, the bread of life and the cup of salvation, the Body and Blood of your Son Jesus Christ.
>
> Grant that all who share this bread and cup may become one body and one spirit, a living sacrifice in Christ, to the praise of your Name.

The epiclesis presents this blessing of bread, wine, and people as the work of the Spirit, and so completes the Trinitarian shape of the Eucharistic prayer. Where the portion before the Sanctus focused on the Creator and the portion after the Sanctus focused on the Jesus as the Word, this final portion focuses on the animation of the assembly for the work of God and the blessing of the bread and wine as food that unites them to Christ and strengthens them for their work. This, really, is the purpose of the Eucharistic prayer, pointing us toward the sending of the church into the world to witness to God's love, a sending that will occur very soon now as the liturgy concludes.

Notably, in Prayer D, the work of the people of God can begin before communion has even been received! After the epiclesis, we may turn once again to intercession. This is not the case in all Eucharistic prayers. But here, prayer for the church to be strengthened for its work is followed by the optional insertion of other prayers as well.

Doxology and Amen. Then the prayer is gathered up in a final Trinitarian summary that reaffirms our trust that our own self-offering and empowerment is made possible through God's own first gift. A "doxology" is, for our purposes here, an act of worship, and this concluding act of worship is followed by the "Great Amen" or "People's Amen."

Though only a single word, the "amen" at the end of the prayer is extremely important and the assembly should utter it with confidence and clarity. It is the bookend to the Sursum Corda that began the prayer with an exchange between priest and people and it affects the nature of the prayer as the work of the whole assembly. Whether the prayer is voiced almost entirely by the priest as representative of the people, or is done in a responsive style with the people and the priest alternating throughout (see Prayer C, for example, BCP p. 369), the Eucharistic prayer is the church's prayer, and it is the whole church that makes its self-offering and its petition for God in Christ to be present in the sacramental food. It is this "amen" to which Augustine referred in our early quotation, encouraging those who eat the meal to "make [their] amen true" by becoming the people of God, themselves broken and poured out for the life of the world in their unity with Christ.

Lord's Prayer. When asked to teach his disciples to pray, Jesus taught the prayer that has become beloved throughout the world and across the centuries. The Lord's Prayer (or "Our Father") is even respected and used by some who are members of religious traditions other than Christianity. The prayer is profound in its directness and simplicity, and while Jesus' teaching of this prayer does not imply that other kinds of prayer are undesirable, it does seem to provide the spirit that ought to live in those other prayers. Jesus (who, we should remember again, was a Jew) first blesses the name of God and prays for the God's heavenly kingdom to be realized in this world, then prays for our basic needs for daily sustenance to be filled as they arise, asks for forgiveness as we ourselves forgive, and for strength to face trials and to be carried by God from the evil that befalls us. As the church fans its desire for God and works to mend the world, it does well to make the heart of its work the simple themes raised here. Whatever else the coming of God's reign will look like, it will be marked by trust, forgiveness, and reliance on God for our strength.

Fraction. The breaking of the bread is a crucial link between what has come before it and what comes after it. Christ has offered his life for us, as we have remembered in the Eucharistic prayer; the breaking of the bread makes it possible for all to share in that life, sacramentalized in the communion of the people. At the same time, if the fraction symbolizes the life of Christ laid down for us, and we ourselves are the Body of Christ, then the fraction becomes a symbol of the shape of our own behavior. We, too, like our crucified and risen Lord, give ourselves to be broken for the life of the world, and find new life in offering ourselves for that breaking.

An anthem or hymn or other formula may be used here. The one most common—"Christ our Passover is sacrificed for us"—links the fraction to the imagery of the Jewish Passover. Both St. Paul and the writer of St. John's gospel used the imagery of Passover to articulate their sense of Jesus Christ as the one through whom the world can pass over from bondage of death to a life of freedom in which worship can be rendered to the God who calls us. Notably, it is that gospel writer who speaks of our path to God not simply by holding intellectual beliefs about Jesus, but being part of him as the "way, truth, and life" (John 14:6). And Paul extends the Passover imagery he uses of Jesus to the church as well (I Cor. 5:7-8). Again, in these biblical writers, we see that the nature of salvation is not simply to believe certain things but to be certain kinds of people: people united to Jesus in his salvific way of life.

Communion. Second to last in the ninefold ordo of the liturgy is the communion of the people. We have actually discussed the meaning of communion by anticipation throughout the earlier pages of this book and will say only a little more here. We eat and drink the sacramental foods. In their transformation as sacramental signs, effected by God in response to prayer, they are an act of receiving the resurrected Jesus' own presence with us. Yet they are just a taste: we receive Christ's presence to us in a world not yet redeemed and we long for a richer feast. Empowered by Christ's presence, united to him most intimately at the table, we prepare to return to a world in which the kingdom is coming but not yet present in abundance. The poor do not eat; the sick are not whole; those relying on riches are cut off through their self-satisfaction from their brothers and sisters and from God; those who hate do violence to others and die themselves in the acids of their own vitriol; those burdened by guilt and afraid of death do not flourish. There is work to be done. And so, after the long build-up of praise, proclamation, and prayer, the high point of the liturgy—the communion of the people—occurs fairly quickly, for its point is not simply consolation but strengthening for mission.

Dismissal. And so, with that in mind, we move promptly to the conclusion of the liturgy. The point of the whole ritual is to sustain us in order to send us. So, following communion, there is a brief prayer of thanksgiving called the "Postcommunion Prayer." In it, we simply give thanks for the sacramental signs of Christ's presence to us, and ask for God to empower and accompany us into the world in witness to God's love. A blessing by the priest is often given but is in some ways redundant, and works best when it connects the blessing we have already received in communion itself with the task of world-mending in God's name that lies before us. The deacon, if present, or the presider, using one of several different options, sends the church into the world. Our response is always: "Thanks be to God."

In some congregations, there is a habit of concluding the liturgy with a processional hymn which, after a brief pause, may be followed by a postlude played by an organist or other musicians. The Prayer Book rubrics really specify that the last of the music will be sung either during the end of communion, just before the postcommunion prayer, or just after it, as a kind of devotional regathering to go forth. Consistent with what we have seen enacted in the structure of the liturgy throughout, the last sound that should ring in the ears of the church as we complete our liturgy is the clear sound of the sending: "Go in peace to love and serve the Lord." The final act of response is completed; proclamation begins again—this time, in the world that God has made and for which Christ lived, died, and rose again.

CHAPTER 4

Bodies in Motion: Gesture, Movement, Ceremonial

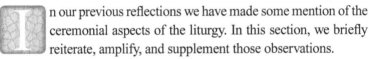n our previous reflections we have made some mention of the ceremonial aspects of the liturgy. In this section, we briefly reiterate, amplify, and supplement those observations.

Liturgy is embodied practice. Movement, gesture, sound, silence, color, and pageantry are all a part of liturgy and not add-ons, even though there is diversity of such practices in evidence. As noted earlier, we are embodied persons—even our cognition is embodied, as today's neuroscience increasingly demonstrates—and the ritual enactment of belief incarnates theology, reshapes our desires, and enacts our transformation at every level of our embodied nature.

Actions and movements within the liturgy have historically been diverse, from the long view. There was a time, though, even after the Book of Common Prayer 1979 was first adopted, that the range of ceremonial, bodily actions within the liturgy was more narrow, grouped around traditions known as "high church" and "low church" that we inherited from earlier liturgical and ideological contexts. Simplifying this distinction here for the sake of brevity, the former (high church) had a high devotional emphasis on the Sacrament and often used elaborate ceremonial; the latter, low church tradition was more emphatic about the Word (often observing Sunday services with the use of Morning Prayer without any Eucharistic practice) and employed little movement or ceremony by comparison. The differences between the two approaches were theological and not simply a matter of taste. The difference *between* these two was in significant contrast to the similarity *within* each tradition of the typical choices made regarding movement and ceremony. Over thirty years of use of the 1979 Book of Common Prayer returned the Episcopal Church to an older practice, one more dominant in some other Christian traditions: it linked the Sunday and the Eucharist. With other churches involved in a liturgical renewal that was underway by the early twentieth century, the Episcopal Church also deepened in its new book the harmony between Word and Sacrament through the very multilayered patterns of the ordo we have been exploring. The decades-long usage of the 1979 prayer book has smoothed out the contrast in all but a very few regions between "high church" and "low church" and significantly diversified practices from one congregation to the next. Moreover, in any one congregation multiple practices may be seen, in part a result of demographic shifts and geographic mobility. That makes it a far more difficult task today than it was when an earlier version of this book was published to describe the ceremonial practices, gestures, movements, and "body practices" that are woven into the liturgy. Much depends on local custom and tradition in an Episcopal Church united by the Eucharistic centrality of Word and Sacrament. The most we can do here, beyond being mindful of specific rubrics within the BCP, is describe very briefly some of the practices one may see.

Let us begin with the moment before the entrance rite. Members of the congregation may enter the sacred space in silence and offer a brief prayer, kneeling, to ready themselves for worship. Silence was once kept before the liturgy began, but as the gathering is increasingly seen to begin at the moment that the people of God gather before the rite even begins, the practice of keeping silence before the service is gradually disappearing in favor of a more festive time of preparation. Some members of the congregation, when they enter their pew, may bow or even kneel toward the front of the church. If asked, some will describe themselves to be acknowledging the cross as the sign of Christ's sacrifice for us; others will say they were taught to "reverence" the altar where the sacrament will be celebrated; still others, in churches where the blessed sacrament is "reserved" (primarily, in the Episcopal Church, for the communication of the sick), will say that they are reverencing the sacramental presence of Christ. In all cases, these are simply signs of respect for sacred space and, notwithstanding specific Christian language for these practices, they reflect a universal instinct to be reverent and humble in space where we seek to encounter the Holy.

The entrance rite may involve a simple signal for the congregation to stand at the entrance of its leaders without fanfare, or it may entail a more elaborate processional ceremony. The latter will usually involve a cross leading the procession, before which some will bow as it passes, accompanied by torches and followed by the choir, other leaders, and the presider. If the Bishop is present, she or he will preside as the chief priest and pastor of the diocese. In some places, incense may be used and swung over the Altar, Ambo, and Font to prepare the place where worship is to be offered and to set the place apart as sacred (or reinforce it). In some cases the people are censed as well, either at this point or more commonly at the offertory. Censing the people makes great sense in light of all that we have said about making us the healing waters and strengthening sustenance for the world. In either case, the entrance rite enacts the movement toward God that is required to worship, a movement made possible first, as we have seen, by God's movement toward us in Jesus Christ.

The hearing of the Word is done seated. Psalms are typically said or sung seated as well, though uncommonly the congregation may stand. This practice is sometimes tied to whether the psalms are chanted (as they were written to be) or said (as is also permissible). We have mentioned already the reasons behind the choice either to read the gospel lesson from a separate book or from the Bible on the Ambo. If read from the Ambo, the book may be censed, signifying its prominence as a liturgical center and the significance of the Bible's testimony to God's living Word. That censing may occur before all the lessons. More commonly, a separate gospel book may be placed on the altar and processed into the congregation for the reading, either simply or elaborately, by the deacon or priest. This practice would be described by many practitioners as symbolic of God sending the

Word into the world in Jesus Christ. It does, as noted earlier, tend to foreground the idea that the gospel is the most important reading and the lens through which the whole Bible is read.

When the gospel is announced by the deacon or priest, one may see some practitioners bow their heads in reverence, or cross themselves, perhaps on the forehead, lips, and chest. They will often describe the meaning of the practice as an embodied prayer for God to enlighten their minds, guide their speech, and move their hearts with the Word. Few of these practices have official meaning and have only been passed along by custom; however, they are all legitimate and laudable as various ways in which embodied people "bring home the meaning" of the corporate physical acts of liturgy in physical acts of their own that link to the larger rite. The gospel may also be censed before its reading, signaling again the holiness of the text as the Word of God in words, and the holiness of the moment as the people attend to its reading.

In the Creed, it is not unusual to see people bow around these verses: "For us and for our salvation he came down from heaven: by the power of the Holy Spirit he became incarnate from the Virgin Mary, and was made man." The EOW text of the creed takes care to foreground the partnership between Mary and the Holy Spirit while respecting still the initiative of God. This is appropriate to the idea of Mary as the "first disciple" who said yes to the Word of God. The EOW language also makes clear that it is the humanity, not the maleness of Jesus that is savingly significant to us. But in either case, the bowing of the head at these verses marks the mystery of the Incarnation as the center of the Christian message of God's love for the world. Some people will bow out of respect for the divine in Jesus anytime the name of Jesus arises in the liturgy. In the Creed, it is also customary for some to cross themselves at the mention of the resurrection of the dead, signaling that the personal longing for life greater than death is linked to the power of Jesus' resurrection and triumph over death into which Christians enter, by hope, through the waters of baptism.

The Prayers of the People (intercessions) may be offered standing or kneeling, and often this connects to the sense a person has of appropriate bodily posture when addressing God. Standing is a sign of respect; kneeling is a sign of humility. Cross-culturally, both have been recommended practices at various times and places when in the presence of royalty or authority. (In some cultures, the removal of the shoes would also fall within this category of behavior.) Neither standing nor kneeling is more "right," though the corporate feeling awakened by standing—the feeling of being open and connected to those around you—has been increasingly favored, since the prayer book promotes the corporate body as the basic unit of the church's identity.

The same observations about standing and kneeling apply to the Eucharistic prayer. In fact, the rubrics commend standing as the preferred posture in Rite II. Before the Eucharist, the altar may be censed, and during the prayer there are a few gestures that are not uncommon: bowing at the name of Jesus, crossing oneself at the words of institution, or, even more commonly, at the Benedictus ("Blessed is he who comes in the name of the Lord") or epiclesis. The words of the Benedictus refer to the coming of Jesus; yet there is a deep instinct at work in this practice, consistent with the meaning of the Eucharist that we have presented in these pages. For those who follow Jesus and seek, through communion, to be made one with him in a fashion described by Augustine and Taft earlier in this book, there is something fundamentally right about crossing oneself at these words; for indeed, it is the church now, united to Christ in the Eucharist, that comes in Christ's name to the world for which he lived and died. At the epiclesis, where the Spirit is asked to bless the people, many will cross themselves to connect themselves bodily with the prayer being voiced at the altar. The fact that the prayer book requires the presider to handle the bread and wine at the recitation of Jesus' words, but does not prescribe any gestures at the epiclesis reflects a preoccupation in the west with those words of institution that need not detain us here; but, consistent with the greater emphasis in the eastern churches on the epiclesis, many presiders in the Episcopal Church will now make some gesture at the epiclesis that enfolds the people in the words of invocation being said. It is natural, then, to see people cross themselves at the same moment out of an instinct to confirm that invocation of God's empowering Spirit on them.

Overall movement depends heavily on the architectural space in which the liturgy occurs. Most commonly, the entire congregation gathers in the nave (the area of the church where the congregation sits) and the leaders will be seated at or near the altar (the chancel or sanctuary, depending on the building). In some sufficiently spacious churches, the "plane" of the altar will not be broken until the time of the offertory and initial preparation of the bread and wine for the Eucharistic prayer and communion; instead, everything up to that point will be led from the floor in front of the nave or from the side. In other places, the entire liturgy will be led from the altar. A number of congregations have had the luxury of building sacred space since the liturgical movement of the twentieth century. In a few such spaces, where the baptismal font sits in a spacious entrance room adjoining the nave, the entire congregation might gather at the font and process into the nave at the entrance rite, and, space still allowing, may even move together to surround the altar for the Eucharistic prayer and communion.

These are a few examples of the behaviors and spatial arrangements that one will see in the liturgy. A participant puzzled and interested by the practices of a particular congregation should always feel free to ask other members of the congregation or the local clergy about anything they would like to understand. Too, the instincts of the body should be followed, as bodies have their own "knowledge." Against the modern inclination to see gesture and movement as expressive of some prior concept, there is nothing wrong with entering into a bodily practice to which one is drawn by the enacted logic and flow of the liturgical rite and seeking to understand afterwards why the body leads one in this particular way.

CONCLUSION

We have considered many liturgical matters here and left out or glossed over many more. But liturgy is fundamentally practice. All the words in a book, whether a short one like this or a thousand page encyclopedia, can only go so far to illuminate what we do when we ritualize. The liturgical action of the church, no less than the puja of Hindus or the meditation and sutra chanting of Buddhists, is a way of inhabiting the world that is not reducible to *thinking* or *talking about* how the world should be, or having ideas about what God or ultimate reality is like. Liturgy is not reducible to words about the liturgy, certainly not to the words of this book the reader now holds; its meaning is found in its doing, and what it does is rehearse a way of being a human being before God. Still, reflections on the experience of liturgy can be helpful to liturgical practice, if the purpose of those words is to reinform and deepen the experience of the liturgy itself, and it is to that end that this book is written. Thus, a few final words of conclusion.

To say that liturgy is a rehearsal of a way of being a human being before God should not mislead. Liturgy is not a *mere* rehearsal; it is the actual, true practice of that way of being that is crystallized there. It is a rehearsal in the sense of recalling us to the rest of life as it ought to be. In truth, all of life is one liturgy, the liturgy that is Jesus Christ, in whom God's whole creation is centered and in whom the world is mended. To enter into that liturgy in all of one's doings and find wholeness there is the point of the liturgy we do on Sundays.

What we have seen is that Christian liturgy does what it does through a combination of content and structure. There are things we say each week, through word and song, but plenty of things we say that change. The *structure* of the liturgy is the skeleton of the ritual body, deepening our connection to God and our identity as the Body of Christ little by little, reshaping our practice to fit our deepest desire for wholeness and redemption, awakening our deep desire for God in the first place. That structure is at once complex and simple: a ninefold ordo containing a threefold Eucharistic prayer in a twofold, constantly recurring pattern of proclamation and response, all overlapping and interacting to reorder our way of seeing and being in the light of the triune God's great love for us. To put the metaphor differently, the structure of the liturgy, its ordo, is not unlike the mask donned by the young man in our opening story. The mask structured his behavior to fit that which he desired; the ordo structures ours. Of course, the ordo is not magic. The young man awakened to the deep desire of his heart. The ordo will not "take us there" without us. But if we can bring to mind and body our own longing for God even a little—our desire to be mended and to find that which mends the world—and bring it repeatedly and honestly to liturgical practice, the liturgical ordo can reshape our behavior over time. The liturgy is not the only place that God leads us to this transformation toward life. But the God who loves and leads and seeks us out in every place and time will surely seek and lead us there.

REFERENCES

1. Alexander Schmemann, *For the Life of the World* (Crestwood, NY: St. Vladimir's, 1976), 26.

2. Robert Taft, "What Does Liturgy Do? Toward a Soteriology of Liturgical Celebration: Some Theses," in *Primary Sources of Liturgical Theology*, ed. Dwight Vogel (Collegeville: Liturgical Press, 2000), 139.

3. Augustine, "Sermon 272," in *The Works of St. Augustine*, Vol. III/7, trans. Edmund Hill (New Rochelle: New City Press, 1993), 300–301.

4. Robert Taft, "What Does Liturgy Do?" 143–44.

5. Nicholas Wolterstorff, "God Everlasting," reprinted in *Ten Essential Texts in the Philosophy of Religion,* ed. by Steven M. Cahn (New York: Oxford University Press, 2005), 57–66.